OUR AMAZING WORLD

MARSUPIALS

Kay de Silva

Aurora

Contents

A wild Red Kangaroo bounding across a nature reserve in Australia.

MARSUPIALS

Marsupials (ma-soo-pi-uls) are commonly known as _pouched mammals._ This is because most marsupials have pouches.

Marsupials are different from other mammals, mainly because they give birth to young that are not fully developed. Those that have pouches use them to nurture their young.

Habitat

Australia, New Guinea, and its nearby islands are home to hundreds of different *species* or types of marsupials. Marsupials, however, are not found only in these parts of the world.

About 70 species of marsupials live in Central and South America. The *Virginia Opossum* is the only species found in North America.

Some marsupials live in grasslands and the forest floor. Others live in underground burrows.

A Virginia Opossum makes a hollowed-out log its home.

ANATOMY

Marsupials range in size. *Red Kangaroos* are the largest marsupials. Adults may measure about 10 feet (3 meters) from their heads to the tip of their tails. *Planigales* are the smallest marsupials. They are about 4 inches (10 centimeters) long, just about the size of a credit card.

A marsupial's pouch is known as a *marsupium*. Not all marsupials, however, have pouches. The presence of the pouch depends on the species. In these species it is the females that have a pouch.

Koalas and kangaroos have well developed pouches. In some species it is just a small fold of skin. Others such as *Marsupial Mice* and *Shrew Opossums* do not have pouches.

Peek-a-boo: A kangaroo joey peers shyly from its mother's pouch.

FEEDING

Most marsupials are *nocturnal* animals. This means that they sleep during the day and are active at night. So they hunt or find food at night. Different marsupials eat different foods.

Most marsupials such as kangaroos and *potoroos* are *herbivores*. These animals eat only plant-based foods. Some species such as *Tasmanian Devils* are carnivores or meat eaters. They may even eat other marsupials such as *wombats*.

Then there are those marsupials that may eat anything they can find. They are known as *omnivores*.

Some marsupials will eat only one kind of food. They are called *specialists*. The *Marsupial Mole* is a *specialist carnivore*. It is known as an *insectivore*, as it eats only ants and termites. Koalas are *specialist herbivores* and eat only the leaves and barks of *eucalyptus* trees.

A kangaroo quenching its thirst at a billabong.

A marsupial mother dedicates her life to protecting her offspring.

PREGNANCY

Most marsupials have a short *gestation period*. This means that the young marsupials grow inside their mothers for a very short time. Virginia Opossums have the shortest gestation period, which is about 12 to 13 days.

Marsupials usually have small *litters*. Larger species such as kangaroos, koalas, wombats, and *wallabies* usually have one offspring. They sometimes have twins. Virginia Opossums, however, usually have about 6 to 10 young.

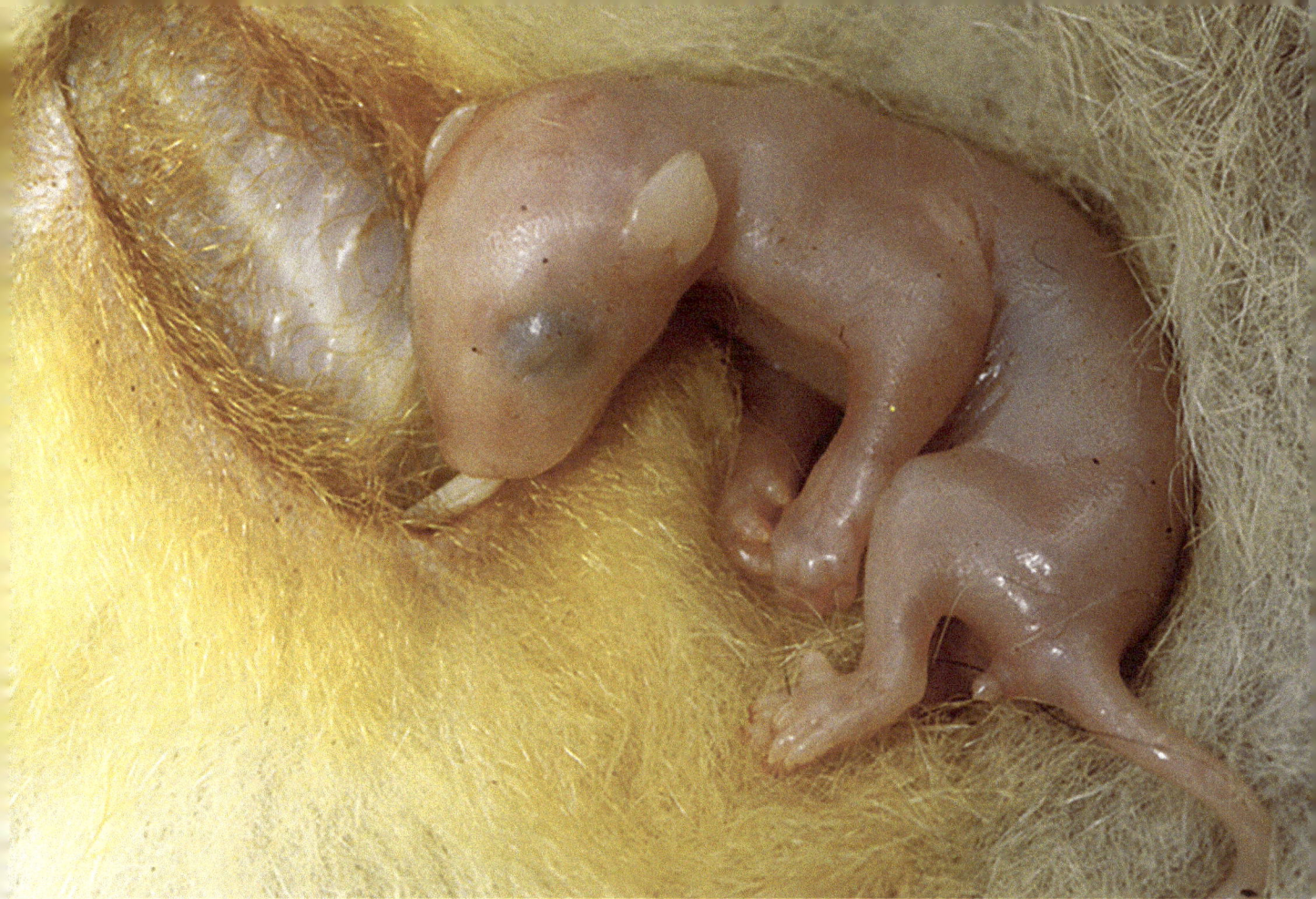

A closeup of a newborn marsupial.

INFANT CARE

Baby marsupials are called *joeys*. *Infant joeys* are born furless and are deaf and blind. Their front limbs, however, are more developed than the rest of their bodies.

This allows them to quickly crawl across their mother's body and latch onto her teats as soon as they are born. In the case of pouched marsupials, these nipples are located inside their mother's pouch.

Some babies remain attached for weeks and even months. Constantly getting milk in this way, they grow safe and warm close to their mothers.

GROWING PAINS

When joeys are fully furred and grown, they go out on their own to find food. As they grow older they increase the time they spend outside the pouch. They will, however, return to their mothers' pouches from time to time.

Once they outgrow the marsupium, some species continue to cling on to some part of their mother's body. Much like children, young marsupials love to spend time with their mother. They go to her in search of rest, comfort, and protection.

A mother opossum giving her full-grown joeys a piggyback ride.

BILBY

The *bilby* is a marsupial that is about the size of a rabbit. It lives in the desserts and dry regions of Australia.

The bilby uses its powerful, clawed limbs to dig deep burrows. It spends the day in these burrows to protect itself from the scorching dessert sun and predators. Under the cover of darkness it quietly leaves its burrow to find food.

It eats anything that it can sink its teeth into. This includes fruits, grubs, insects, spiders, and fungi. Like the koala, it gets most of its water from the food that it eats.

A bilby foraging in sand for food.

A Brushtail Possum chowing down on a mango.

COMMON BRUSTHTAIL POSSUM

The *Common Brushtail Possum* gets its name from its brush-like tail. It uses its tail to grip tree branches.

This possum is one of 70 species of possums. It is commonly found in Australia and New Zealand. Its natural habitats are *eucalyptus* and tropical rainforests. It is, however, quite comfortable around humans, so it is frequently found living in the city.

Like most possums, it spends the day sleeping and the night prowling for food. It enjoys leaves, fruits, and flowers.

A pair of quolls huddling together in a hollow log.

EASTERN QUOLL

The *Eastern Quoll* is a marsupial that lives in Australia and New Guinea. It is about 2 feet (60 centimeters) long and weighs 3 pounds (1.3 kilograms).

The Eastern Quoll is a carnivore. It spends its nights looking for food on the forest floor. It mostly eats insects. It also enjoys mice, rabbit, and *carrion*. Carrion is the rotting remains of animal flesh.

During the day it rests under a burrow of rocks or in a hollow log.

KANGAROO

The kangaroo is possibly the best known marsupial in the world. It is found in Australia and New Guinea.

The kangaroo is the largest member of the *Macropod* family. Macropod means with great big feet. As this name suggests, it has powerful hind legs and large feet. These help it travel across great distances. A kangaroo can move as fast as 40 mph (miles per hour). This is as fast as a racehorse.

It can also leap up to 30 feet (9 meters) high. It uses its long and muscular tail to help keep its balance as it jumps.

Although kangaroos look friendly, they can be dangerous if threatened. They are known to first stamp their large feet in warning. Then they use their strong feet to kick and fight. They are also known to bite sometimes.

In Eastern Australia Kangaroos are found living in herds. These groups are also called mobs. Mother kangaroos carry their joeys in their pouches. At birth the infant is just about the size of a grape.

A kangaroo with a joey in her pouch staring intently at the camera.

KOALA

The koala lives in Eastern and Southern Australia. The koala is a marsupial. It is, however, often mistaken for a bear. Its thick, woolly coat protects it from the heat and cold. It also acts like a raincoat to keep it dry.

Rarely found on the ground, this tree-dwelling marsupial is often found eating or sleeping in a eucalyptus tree. It has rough pads on its hands and feet that it uses to climb trees. Much like the *Panda Bear*, the koala has five clawed fingers to grip eucalyptus trees.

The koala is a very fussy eater. An herbivorous specialist, it eats only from some eucalyptus trees. It spends many hours at night munching on eucalyptus. The leaves and bark of these trees are not very nourishing and are difficult to digest. So when it is not eating, the koala sleeps or lies very still for up to 16 hours at a time.

An infant koala joey is the size of a jelly bean when it crawls into its mother's pouch. Its first food is its mother's milk. Then its mother feeds it pap from her *intestines*. This gives the joey the *bacteria* it needs to digest the tough eucalyptus.

A koala snoozing in a gum tree, Sydney, Australia.

Numbat

The *numbat* is a marsupial that is found in the forests of Western Australia. The numbat is different from most marsupials because it does not have a pouch. It is also diurnal. This means that it is most active during the day. It spends the night resting inside a hollow log.

Like the koala, it, too, is a specialist eater. The numbat is also called the *Banded Ant Eater*. Can you guess what it eats? It eats only termites! This tiny creature that is just a bit longer than a foot ruler eats 20,000 termites every day.

It does not have strong claws, like other ant-eating mammals, to tear termite colonies apart, so it uses its pointed nose to sniff out corridors used by termites. It then snaps the insects up using its long sticky tongue.

An extremely rare capture of a numbat.

A potoroo looks like a bandicoot and hops like a kangaroo!

POTOROO

The _potoroo_ is a marsupial that is found in Southeastern Australia. It is also called the _Rat Kangaroo_. This is because the potoroo looks like a kangaroo that is the size of a rat.

Like a kangaroo, the potoroo has powerful hind legs that it uses to hop from place to place. The potoroo is also a nocturnal marsupial like the kangaroo. Unlike the herbivorous kangaroo, however, the potoroo is an omnivore. Its favorite food is _truffles_, which is a type of fungi. It may also eat seeds and insects.

A curious Quokka in the wilderness at daybreak.

QUOKKA

The *quokka* is a marsupial that looks like a tiny kangaroo. It is about 3 feet (1 meter) long. Just like a kangaroo, the quokka has very powerful hind legs.

These marsupials are social creatures. During the day they sleep in family groups in burrows. They gather in large groups at *billabongs* or watering holes at night. These animals enjoy grass, seeds, and leaves.

SUGAR GLIDER

The *Sugar Glider* is found in Australia, its nearby islands, New Guinea, and Indonesia. It lives in trees and rarely touches the ground.

It moves from tree to tree, but does not have wings. Instead it has a thin layer of skin called a *patagium*, which it uses to glide. The patagium is attached to it wrists and ankles. When it is ready to glide, it spreads out its limbs and descends like a parachute. It uses its legs and long tail to steer itself in the right direction.

A fully-grown Sugar Glider weighs about 4 ounces (100 grams). This is about the weight of two chicken eggs. Its entire body, including its tail, is about the length of a foot ruler. It can, however, glide over 150 feet (45 metres).

The Sugar Glider is an omnivore whose favorite foods are fruits and vegetables. It also enjoys tree sap, nectar, pollen, and a variety of *arthropods*. It gets its name from its love of sweet foods.

A Sugar Glider preparing to take flight.

TASMANIAN DEVIL

The *Tasmanian Devil* is mostly found in the dry eucalyptus forests of Tasmania. It is about 2.5 feet (75 centimeters) long and weighs up to 26 pounds (12 kilograms). This marsupial has a large head, a long snout, and a muscular body.

It has very powerful jaws and large teeth. It is the largest carnivorous marsupial in the world. It is also the hardest biting carnivore on the face of the planet.

The Tasmanian Devil is known as a somewhat lazy *predator*. It is more of a *scavenger* than a hunter and is happy to eat carrion. When it must hunt it will attack anything it can sink its teeth into. This includes kangaroos and other marsupials, reptiles, birds, and fish.

Long ago, natives feared this animal because of the screeching sounds it makes when it eats. This is why it is known as the *devil*.

A snarling Tassie-Devil poised to attack.

VIRGINIA OPOSSUM

The Virginia Opossum is the only marsupial that lives in North America. It usually stays in a hollow log or abandoned rodent burrow.

It forages for food at night. It is an omnivore that enjoys feeding on fruits, leaves, seeds, insects, lizards, snails, and pretty much anything it can find.

There are many animals that are known for their amazing ability to move and for their extraordinary physical feats. The Virginia Opossum, however, is best known for its ability to stay very still.

If this creature is attacked, it hisses and shows its sharp teeth to scare away its attacker. If this does not work, it just pretends to be dead. To do this it rolls over, goes stiff, and hangs its tongue out. Then it remains perfectly still until its attacker loses interest and walks away.

Have you ever pretended to be asleep when a grownup has tried to wake you to go to school? Well, if you have, you have *played possum.*

"Playing Possum": A Virginia Opossum playing dead.

A mob of Yellow-footed Rock Wallabies in their natural habitat.

WALLABY

The wallaby is a member of the macropod family. Wallaby is the name given to an animal that is not big enough to be called a kangaroo. There are about 30 species of wallabies.

Wallabies are found in Australia and its nearby islands. Most Wallaby species are grouped according to their habitat, so there are *Rock Wallabies*, *Brush Wallabies*, and *Shrub Wallabies*.

Like all macropods, a wallaby has a pair of strong legs and big feet that it hops around on. It uses its stocky tail to keep its balance.

Like the kangaroo, the wallaby is herbivorous. It usually eats grasses and leaves.

A close encounter with a Wombat in a national park in Australia.

WOMBAT

The wombat is found in Australia and its nearby islands. It has powerful legs and sharp claws. It uses these to build burrows in eucalyptus forests and grasslands. The wombat is known as the largest burrowing animal on earth.

The *Common Wombat* likes to live alone in its own burrow. Other species are more social. They often live together in large groups called colonies. These colonies live in underground cities. The cities are made up of several chambers and corridors.

The wombat is an herbivore. At night it comes out of its burrow to dine on grasses, leaves, bark, and roots.

A young orphaned Brushtail Possum hand-reared after being rescued.

MARSUPIALS IN TROUBLE

Marsupials are interesting and loveable creatures. Like many *endangered* animals, however, they are fast disappearing from our planet. This is called *extinction*.

Animals become extinct mainly because of human activity such as *deforestation*. Deforestation robs animals of their natural habitat, which provides them with food and shelter.

Conservationists work on protecting animals and their habitats. You can be a conservationist, too, by taking care of our environment and being kind to all living creatures.

Our Amazing World

COLLECT THEM ALL

WWW.OURAMAZINGWORLDBOOKS.COM

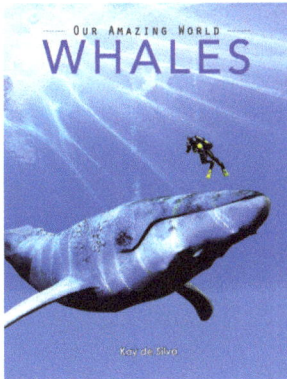

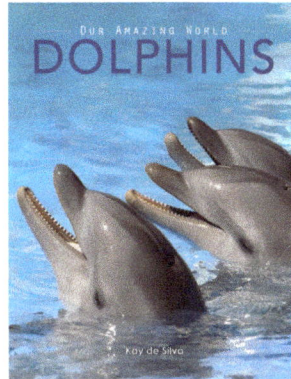

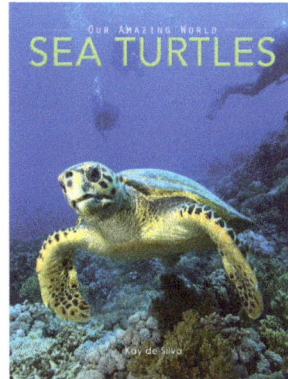

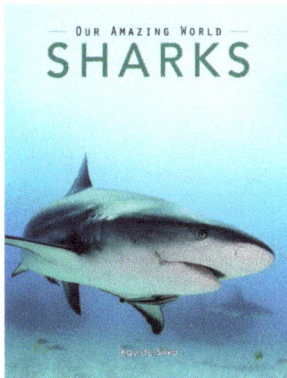

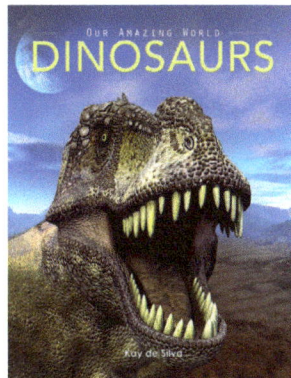

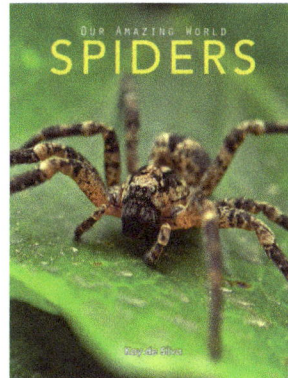

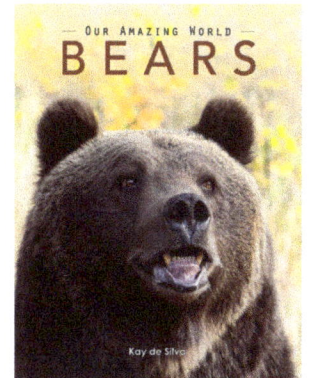

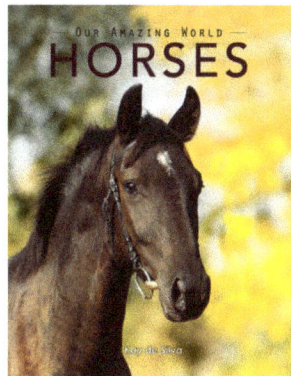

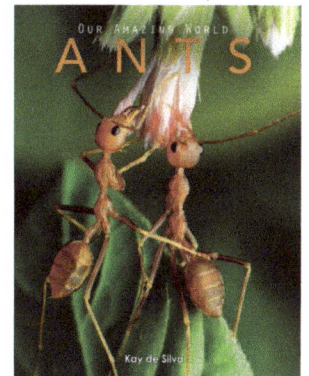

OUR AMAZING WORLD
WHALES
Kay de Silva

DOLPHINS
Kay de Silva

OUR AMAZING WORLD
SEA TURTLES
Kay de Silva

OUR AMAZING WORLD
PENGUINS
Kay de Silva

OUR AMAZING WORLD
SHARKS
Kay de Silva

OUR AMAZING WORLD
DINOSAURS
Kay de Silva

OUR AMAZING WORLD
SPIDERS
Kay de Silva

OUR AMAZING WORLD
BEARS
Kay de Silva

OUR AMAZING WORLD
POLAR BEARS
Kay de Silva

OUR AMAZING WORLD
HORSES
Kay de Silva

OUR AMAZING WORLD
TIGERS
Kay de Silva

OUR AMAZING WORLD
ANTS
Kay de Silva

PRINT
BOOK
GIVEAWAY

ENTER NOW

OURAMAZINGWORLDBOOKS.COM

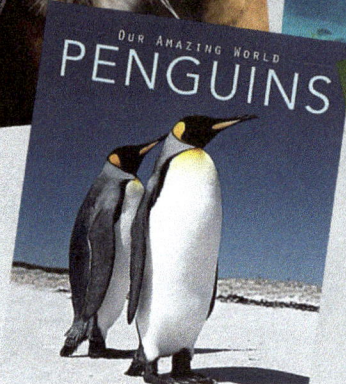

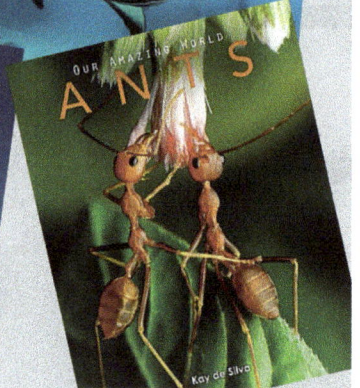

OUR AMAZING WORLD
TIGERS

OUR AMAZING WORLD
SHARKS

OUR AMAZING WORLD
PENGUINS

OUR AMAZING WORLD
ANTS

Kay de Silva

Aurora
An imprint of CKTY Publishing Solutions

ouramazingworldbooks.com

Text copyright © Kay de Silva, 2013
The moral right of the author has been asserted

ISBN 978-0-9946009-5-0

shutterstock.com